A Patriotic Devotional

B.B. Gould

"Blessed is the Nation whose God is the Lord"

Psalms 33:12

Cover Portrait: "The Prayer at Valley Forge by Arnold Friberg is one of the best known paintings of the American Revolution. It depicts George Washington at Valley Forge, Pennsylvania in prayer on his knees beside his horse Nelson at the Continental Army's encampment, during the terrible winter of 1777-1778."

http://www.revolutionary-war-and-beyond.com/prayer-at-valley-forge-2.html

The DAR Insignia is the property of, and is copyrighted by, the National Society of the Daughters of the American Revolution.

Copyright © 2014

Bicentennial Edition, 1976

Revised Edition, 2014
Published by
Hawk & Hummingbird Press

Miami, Florida

Table of Contents

Forward..4

God..5-15

Home..16-23

Country...24-35

Scriptures of the Presidents General......................36-37

Our Florida State Regents..................................38-39

In Memory..40

Our Chaplain General..41

Acknowledgments..42

About the Author...43

Forward

My maternal grandmother, Ruby Maude Brown Pinkston, inspired me to write prayers and affirmations at an early age. She was a charter member of the Golden Anchor Chapter, North Miami Beach, Florida, and served as its first chaplain.

In the Bicentennial year of 1976 my mother, Stella Elvira Pinkston "Pinkie" Hamlin, encouraged me to form a committee to commemorate the 200th birthday of our country. It was an exciting time to be regent. Carole Broom Melendez served as chairman of the committee and created an inspiring collection of writings of the founding fathers and mothers. She called it "A Patriotic Devotional."

Thirty eight years later I am fortunate to serve as regent of the Biscayne Chapter and present a revised edition of "A Patriotic Devotional." It has been updated to include the scriptures of the Presidents General from 1976 to the present and many of the Florida State Regent's scriptures and themes. Like the motto of the National Society, Daughters of the American Revolution, this devotional is divided into three sections to represent "God, Home and Country."

It is my hope to share with you the spirit of the original patriotic devotional. May you find comfort in the pages.

God

George Washington's Prayer for His Country

Bless our land with honorable industry, sound learning, and pure manners. Save us from violence, discord and confusion; from pride and arrogancy and from every evil way.

Defend our liberties and fashion into one united people the multitude brought out of many kindreds and tongues. Endue with the spirit of wisdom those whom in Thy name we entrust the authority of government, that there be peace and justice at home, and that through obedience to Thy law, we may show forth Thy praise among the nations of the earth. Amen.

"Work as if everything depended on you,
and pray as if everything depended on God."
St. Augustine

God

On Independence
Author Unknown

Come all you brave soldiers, both valiant and free,
It's for independence we all now agree;
Let us gird on our swords, and prepare to defend
Our liberty, property, ourselves and our friends.

In a cause that's so righteous, come let us agree,
And from hostile invaders set America free,
The cause is so glorious we need not to fear,
But from merciless tyrants we'll set ourselves clear.

Heaven's blessing attending us, no tyrant shall say
That American e'er to such monsters gave way,
But fighting we'll die in America's cause,
Before we'll submit to tyrannical laws.

God

May heaven's blessings descend on our United States,
And grant that the union may never abate,
May love, peace and harmony ever be found,
For to go hand in hand America round.

Upon our grand congress, may heaven bestow
Both wisdom and skill our good to pursue,
On heaven alone, dependent we'll be,
But from all earthly tyrants we mean to be free.

May heaven smile on us in all our endeavors,
Safe guard our seaports, our towns and our rivers,
Keep us from invaders by land and by sea,
And from all who'd deprive us of our liberty.

God

Nathaniel Niles
"Bunker Hill or The American Hero"
(The first four stanzas of the most widely sung of
Revolutionary songs, 1775)

Why should vain mortals tremble at the sight of
Death and destruction in the field of battle,
Where blood and carnage clothe the ground in crimson,
Sounding with death-groans?

Death will invade us by the means appointed,
And we must all bow to the king of terrors;
Nor am I anxious, if I am prepared,
What shape he comes in.

Infinite goodness teaches us submission;
Bids us be quiet under all His dealings;
Never repining, but forever praising
God our creator.

God

Well may we praise Him, all his ways are perfect;
Though a resplendence infinitely glowing
Dazzles in glory on the sight of mortals,
Struck blind by luster!

"Guard that which is committed to thy trust."
1 Timothy 6:20

God

A Revolutionary War Hymn

Then did they to Jehovah cry
When they were in distress,
Who did them set at liberty
Out of their anguishes.

In such a way that was most right
He led them forth also,
That to a city which they might
Inhabit they might go.

John Adams' wife later added these cherished words:
This is our day of deliverance,
With solemn acts of devotion to God,
We ought to commemorate it
From this time forevermore.

God

July 19, 1776

On this day, Independence was proclaimed in Boston.

John Adams, while sitting in Philadelphia's City Tavern, reading a letter from his wife, was reminded of his own words:

"I am well aware of the toil and blood and treasure it will cost us to maintain this declaration and support and defend these states. Yet through all the gloom I can see the rays of ravishing light and glory.

I can see the end is worth all the means. This is our day of deliverance. With solemn acts of devotion to God we ought to commemorate it with pomp and parade, with shows, games, sports, guns, bells, bonfires and illuminations from one end of the continent to the other, from this time forward forevermore."

"Yea, I have a goodly heritage."
Psalms 16:6

God

James Madison
Virginia Journal, 1776

That religion, or the duty which we owe to our Creator, and the manner of discharging it, can be directed only by reason and conviction, not by force or violence.

And, therefore, that all men should enjoy the fullest toleration in the exercise of religion, according to the dictates of conscience, unpunished, and unrestrained by the magistrate, unless under color of religion any man disturb the peace, the happiness, or safety of society. And that it is the mutual duty of all to practice Christian forbearance, love and charity towards each other.

"Thou shalt remember all the way which the Lord thy God hath led thee."

Deuteronomy 8:2

God

Francis Salvador
1747-1776

Francis Salvador was the first Jew in South Carolina to hold public office and to die for American independence.

He came to Charles Town, from his native London in 1773 to develop extensive family land-holdings in the frontier district of Ninety Six. As a deputy to the Provincial Congresses of South Carolina, 1775 and 1776, he served with distinction in the creation of this state and nation.

Participating as a volunteer in an expedition against Indians and Tories, he was killed from ambush near the Keowee River, August 1, 1776.

Born an aristocrat, he became a democrat: an Englishman, he cast his lot with America; true to his ancient faith, he gave his life for new hopes of human liberty and understanding.

(From a commemorative plaque, erected in 1950, approved by the Historical Commission, Charleston, S.C.)

God

John Jay's Charge to the Grand Jury
Ulster County, New York, 1777

The Americans are the first people who heaven favored with an opportunity of deliberating upon, and choosing the forms of government under which they should live.

All other constitutions have derived their existence from violence or accidental circumstances, and are, therefore, probably more distant from their perfection, which, though beyond our reach, may nevertheless be approached under the guidance of reason and experience.

"Blessed is the nation whose God is the Lord."
Psalms 33:12

God

President George Washington
A Portion of the Farewell Address — September 19, 1796

Of all the dispositions and habits which lead to political prosperity, religion and morality are indispensable supports. In vain would that man claim the tribute of patriotism, who should labor to subvert these great pillars of human happiness, these firmest props of the duties of men and citizens.

The mere politician equally with the pious man ought to respect and to cherish them. A volume could not trace all their connections private and public felicity. Let it simply be asked where is the security for property, for reputation, for life, if the sense of religious obligation deserts the oaths, which are the instruments of investigation in courts of justice?

And let us with caution indulge the supposition that morality can be maintained without religion. Whatever may be conceded to the influence of refined education on minds of peculiar structure, reason and experience both forbid us to expect that national morality can prevail in exclusion of religious principle.

Home

Benjamin Church

Come join hand in hand, brave Americans all,
And rouse your bold hearts at fair Liberty's call;
No tyrannous acts shall suppress your just claim,
Or stain with dishonor America's name.

Our worthy forefathers, let's give 'em a cheer
To climates unknown did courageously steer;
Through oceans to deserts for freedom they came,
And dying, bequeathed their freedom and fame.

The tree their own hands had to liberty reared,
They lived to behold growing strong and revered;
With transport they cried, "Now our wishes we gain,
And our children shall gather the fruits of our pain."

Home

This bumper I crown for our sovereign's health,
And this for Britannia's glory and wealth;
That wealth and that glory immortal may be,
If she is but just and if we are but free.

(This song was first sung by John Adams to the people of Boston at a feast given on the anniversary of the first public protest against the Stamp Act, August 14, 1765.)

Come, ye thankful people, come, raise the song of harvest home; all is safely gathered in, ere the winter storms begin. God our maker doth provide for our wants to be supplied; come to God's own temple, come, raise the song of harvest home.

Henry Alford

Mark 4: 26 –29

Home

Thomas Paine
The Crisis   December, 1776

    These are the times that try men's souls: the summer soldier and the sunshine patriot will, in this crisis, shrink from the service of his country; but he that stands it now, deserves the love and thanks of man and woman.

    Tyranny, like hell, is not easily conquered; yet we have this consolation with us, that the harder the conflict the more glorious the triumph.

Our DAR Insignia

(from the DAR website, Insignia Committee)

The Hub — a Daughter's Loyal Heart

Each Spoke — a Thought of Those who Part

The Tire — a Noble Life's Bright Round

Each Star — a Deed in Heaven Profound

Each Flaxen Thread — a Cord of Love

The only jewel in the world
That money cannot buy
Without such proof of ancestry
As no one can deny

Home

William Pitt

Addressing the House of Commons   January, 1776

  The Americans are the sons, not the bastards of England. It's said...The gentleman asks, when were the colonies emancipated?

  But I desire to know, when they were made slaves...

The gentleman tells us, America is obstinate, America is almost in open rebellion.

  I rejoice that America has resisted. Three millions of people so dead to all the feelings of liberty, as voluntarily to submit to be slaves, would have been fit instruments to have made slaves of the rest.

Home

Robert Treat Paine
Jefferson and Liberty

The gloomy night before us flies:
The reign of terror now is o'er,
Its gags, inquisitors and spies,
Its hordes of harpies are no more.

Rejoice! Columbia's sons, rejoice!
To tyrants never bend the knee,
But join with heart, and soul, and voice,
For Jefferson and liberty.

O'er vast Columbia's varied clime,
Her cities, forests, shores and dales,
In rising majesty sublime,
Immortal liberty prevails.

Home

Rejoice! Columbia's sons & Co.

Hail! Long expected glorious day!
Illustrious, memorable morn;
That freedom's fabric from decay
Secures for millions yet unborn.

Rejoice! Columbia's sons & Co.

Rise to Challenges
Relish Experiences
Recognize Opportunities

G.G.'s Principle: Three Steps to Empower You
in Any Situation
2011

Home

Speech of Hesper
The Closing Verse of an Invocation
Constitutional Convention

But know ye favored race one potent head
Must rule your states and strike your foes with dread,
The finance regulate, the trade control,
Live through the empire and accord the whole.

Ere death invades, and night's sleep deep curtain falls,
Through ruined realms the voice of union calls
Loud as the trump of heaven through darkness roars,
When gyral gusts entomb Caribbean towers.
When nature trembles, through the deeps convulsed
And ocean foams from craggy cliffs repulsed.
On you she calls! Attend the warning cry:

Ye live united or divided die!

Home

Benjamin Franklin
Poor Richard's Almanac

Mankind are very odd creatures: one half censure what they practice, the other half practice what they censure; the rest always say and do as they ought.

The good will of the governed will be starved, if not fed by the good deeds of the governors.

Sell not virtue to purchase wealth, nor liberty to purchase power.

Anne Bradstreet
America's First Poet

It is but vain unjustly to wage war,
Men can do best, and women know it well,
Pre-eminence in all and each is yours —
Yet grant some small acknowledgement of ours.

Country

Patrick Henry
March, 1775

Is life so dear, or peace so sweet,
As to be purchased at the price of chains and slavery?
Forbid it, Almighty God!
I know not what course others may take;
But as for me,
Give me liberty or give me death!

Our heavenly father, we thank thee for Thy guidance in the life of our country. Grant us, we pray, growth and understanding. May we always possess the integrity, courage and strength to keep ourselves unshackled, to remain a citadel of freedom and a beacon of hope to all the world. Amen.

Major Francis Langhorne Dade Chapter
Miami, Florida

Country

Crispus Attucks
c. 1723—March 5, 1770

The first person to die for American freedom, Crispus Attucks was a fugitive slave who had worked for twenty years as a merchant seaman.

When Samuel Adams called upon the dock workers and seamen in the port of Boston to demonstrate against the British troops guarding the customs commissioners, forty to fifty patriots, armed with clubs, sticks and snowballs attacked the British troops.

The British troops responded with a barrage of rapid fire. Crispus Attucks was the first to fall in what became known as the "Boston Massacre." Four other Americans died that fatal day of March 5, 1770.

Country

The New Massachusetts Liberty Song
Author Unknown, Virginia Gazette, January 6, 1774

That seat of science Athens and Earth's proud mistress Rome
Where now are all their glories? We scarce find their tomb,
Then guard your rights, Americans, nor stoop to lawless sway,
Oppose, oppose, oppose, oppose for North America.

Proud Albion bowed to Caesar and numberous lords before,
To Picts, to Danes, to Normans, and many masters more;
But we can boast Americans have never fallen prey,
Huzza! Huzza! Huzza! Huzza! for free America.

We led fair freedom hither and lo, the desert smiled
A paradise of pleasure now opened in the wild;
Your harvest, bold Americans, no power shall snatch away,
Preserve, preserve, preserve your rights in free America.

Country

Torn from a world of tyrants, beneath the western sky
We formed a New Dominion, a land of liberty;
The world shall own we're masters here, then hasten on the day,
Huzza! Huzza! Huzza! Huzza! for love and liberty.

God bless this maiden climate, and through her vast domain
May hosts of heroes cluster that scorn to wear a chain,
And blast the venal sycophant who dare our rights betray,
Assert yourselves, yourselves, yourselves for brave America.

Lift up your hearts, my heroes and swear with proud disdain,
The wretch that would ensnare you shall spread his net in vain;
Should Europe empty all her force we'd meet them in array,
And shout Huzza! Huzza! Huzza! for brave America.

Some fitter day shall crown us the masters of the Main,
In giving laws and freedom to subject France and Spain;
And all the isles o'er ocean spread shall tremble and obey,
The lords, the lords, the lords, the lords of North America.

Country

Thomas Paine

Our citizenship in the United States is our national character. Our citizenship in any particular state is only our local distinction.

By the latter we are known at home, by the former to the world. Our great title is Americans.

From the "Ritual for Chapter Meetings"

Our Father in heaven, we thank you for They abiding presence in the life of our country. We thank Thee for all those yesterdays of our human race whose lessons and fulfillments have become a heritage to us.

Continue, we pray, Thy blessings upon this nation that all who are a part of it may learn true nobility of manhood and womanhood.

Grant us growth in understanding and increasing devotion to righteousness. In Thy name we pray.   Amen

Country

Holt's Gazette, 1776
Author Unknown

Cursed be the man who e'er shall raise
His sacrilegious hand,
To drive fair liberty, our praise!
From his own native land.

O may his memory never die,
By future ages cursed;
But live to lasting infamy,
Branded of traitor's worth.

But Happy! Happy! Happy they,
Who in their country's cause
Shall cast reluctant fear away,
Immortal in applause!

Who with their conscious virtue girt,
Shan't dread oppression's voice;
But boldly dare those rights to assert,
In which all men rejoice.

Country

In Response to Unfair Taxation of the Colonies

To all, both land and seamen
Who glory in the day
When we shall all be freemen
In North America,

Success to legislation,
That rules with gentle hand,
To trade and navigation,
By water and by land.

May all with one opinion,
Our wholesome laws obey,
Throughout this vast dominion
Of North America.

Country

John Adams

Government is a simple, intelligent thing, founded in nature and reason, quite comprehensible by common sense…..The true source of all our suffering has been our timidity…..Let us dare to read, think, speak, write.

Let every order and degree among the people arouse. Let the pulpit resound…..Let the bar proclaim…..Let our sluice of knowledge be opened and set a-flowing.

We gather together to ask the Lord's blessing; he chastens and hastens his will to make known. The wicked oppressing now cease from distressing; sing praises to his name; he forgets not His own.

We all do extol thee, thou leader triumphant, and pray that thou still our defender wilt be. Let thy congregation escape tribulation; thy name be ever praised! O Lord, make us free!

1626 *Nederlandtsch Gedencklanck*
trans. by Theodore Baker

Country

John Adams
Defense of the Constitutions of Government of the United States of America, 1788

The world has been too long abused with notions that climate and soil decide the characters and political institutions of nations. The laws of Solom and the despotism of Mahomet have, at different times, prevailed at Athens; consuls, emperors and pontiffs have ruled at Rome. Can there be desired a stronger proof, that policy and education are able to triumph over every disadvantage of climate?

Mankind has been still more injured by insinuations, that a certain celestial virtue, more than human, has been necessary to preserve liberty. Happiness, whether in despotism or democracy, whether in slavery or liberty, can never be found without virtue.

The best republics will be virtuous, and have been so; but we hazard a conjecture, that the virtues have been the effect of the well ordered constitution, rather than the cause. And, perhaps, it would be impossible to prove that a republic cannot exist even among highwaymen, by setting one rogue to watch another; and the knaves themselves may in time be made honest men by the struggle.

Country

Joel Barlow

"Hymn to Peace"

Read with emotion by the members of Congress in celebration of the treaty with England after seven years of war.

From scenes of blood, these beauteous shores that stain

From gasping friends that press the sanguine plain,

From fields, long taught in vain they flight to mourn,

I rise, delightful power, and greet thy glad return.

Too long the groans of death, and battle's bray

Have rung discordant through the unpleasing lay;

Let pity's tear its balmy fragrance shed,

O'er heroes' wounds and patriot warriors dead;

Accept, departed shades, these grateful sighs

Your fond attendants to the approving skies.

Country

President George Washington
September 19, 1796
A Portion of the Farewell Address

Observe good faith and justice towards all nations. Cultivate peace and harmony with all. Religion and morality enjoin this conduct; and can it be that good policy does not equally enjoin it?

It will be worthy of a free, enlightened, and at no distant period, a great nation to give to mankind the magnanimous and too novel example of a people always guided by an exalted justice and benevolence.

Who can doubt that in the course of time and things the fruit of such a plan would richly repay any temporary advantages which might be lost by a steady adherence to it?

Country

Iroquois Thanksgiving Ritual

Now we will speak again, Our Creator. He decided, "Above the world I have created...I will continue to look intently and to listen intently to the earth, when people direct their voices at me."

Let there be gratitude day and night for the happiness He has given us. He loves us, He who in the sky dwells. He gave us the means to set right that which divides us.

Seneca
Handsome Lake

Love one another and do not strive for another's undoing. Even as you desire good treatment, so render it.

Muscogee Creek
Heleluyan!

Scriptures of the Presidents General

Sara R. Jones (1974-1975) - "Whatsoever Thy hand findeth to do, do it with Thy might." Ecclesiastes 9:10

Jane F. Smith (1975-1977) - "All things work together for good to them that love God..." Romans 8:28
"Remove not the ancient landmark which thy fathers have set." Proverbs 22:28

Jeannette O. Baylies (1977-1980) - "The way of the Lord is strength to the upright." Proverbs 10:29

Patricia W. Shelby (1980-1983) - "For we are laborers together with God." Corinthians 3:9
"And now abideth faith, hope, love, these three; but the greatest of these is love." 1 Corinthians 13:13

Sarah M. King (1983-1986) - "In everything you do, put God first and He will direct you, and crown your efforts with success." Proverbs 3:6

Ann D. Fleck (1986-1989) - (Taken from her speeches) "Be ye doers of the word, and not hearers only..." James 1:22

Marie H. Yochim (1989-1992) - "Blest Be the Tie That Binds" Hymn

Wayne G. Blair (1992-1995) - "Guard that which is committed to thy trust." 1 Timothy 6:20

Dorla Dean Kemper (1995-1998) - "Lord, lift thou up the light of Thy countenance upon us." Psalm 4:6b
"I know thy works: behold, I have set before thee an open door, and no man can shut it." Revelations 3:8

Georgeane F. Love (1998-2001) - "And beyond all these things put on love, which is the perfect bond of unity." Colossians 3:14

Linda T. Watkins (2001-2004) - "And the tree of the field shall yield her fruit, and the earth shall yield the increase, and they shall be safe in their land." Ezekiel 34:27

Presley M. Wagoner (2004-2007) - "Now the Lord is the spirit, and where the spirit of the Lord is, there is freedom." 2 Corinthians 3:17
"Make a joyful noise unto the Lord, all ye lands." Psalm 100

Linda G. Calvin (2007-2010) - "Be hospitable to one another." 1 Peter 4:9
"Encourage one another and build each other up." 1 Thessalonians 5:11

Merry Ann T. Wright (2010-2013) - "And now abideth faith, hope, and love, these three; but the greatest of these is love." 1 Corinthians 13:13
"What does the Lord require of you but to do justice, to love mercy, and to walk humbly with your God." Micah 6:8

Lynn F. Young (2013-2016) - "He will cover you with his feathers, and under his wing you will find refuge; his faithfulness will be your shield and rampart." Psalm 91:4
"Guard that which is committed to thy trust." 1 Timothy 6:20

Our Florida State Regents

Cynthia Wolfe Symanek (2013-2015) — "Let us not grow weary in doing good, for at the proper time we will reap a harvest if we do not give up." Galatians 6:9

Donna Griffin Cullen (2011-2013) — "Therefore encourage one another and build up each other, as indeed you are doing." 1 Thessalonians 5:11

Barbara Whalin Makant (2009-2011) — "Above all, clothe yourselves with love, which binds everything together in perfect harmony." Colossians 3:14

Sue Chenault Bratton (2007-2009) — "To the heavens I shall go up, above the stars of God." Isaiah 14:13

Rebecca Ellington Lockhart (2005-2007) — "Delight yourself in the Lord; and He will give you the desires of your heart." Psalms 37:4

Jean Dixon Mann (2003-2005) — "Let your light shine before men, so that they may see your good works." Matthew 5:16

Mary Lou Clutter James (2001-2003) — "Trust in God and flourish like a tree." Proverbs 11:28

Jeannette Joiner Frey (1999-2001) — "This is the day which the Lord has made; let us rejoice and be glad in it." Psalms 118:24

Aida Thomas Register (1997-1999) — "Stars" - a favorite symbol during her administration: "You are a child of the universe, no less than the trees and the stars." — Max Ehrmann

Anne White Stewart (1995-1997) — "Success" was one of her themes: "A ship in harbor is safe, but that is not what ships are built for." — John A. Shedd

Ruth Dennis McGarity (1992-1995) — "Peace Prayer of St. Francis"

Lord, make me an instrument of your peace. Where there is hatred, let me sow love; where there is injury, pardon; where there is doubt, faith; where there is despair, hope; where there is darkness, light; and where there is sadness, joy. O Divine Master, grant that I may not so much seek to be consoled, as to console; to be understood, as to understand; to be loved, as to love. For it is in giving that we receive, it is in pardoning that we are pardoned, and it is in dying that we are born to Eternal Life. Amen.

In Memory

Edith Smith Kimbell
Chaplain General, 1932-1935
(from the original DAR Ritual)

      Grant that we may live a patriotism of willing service; that we may love our country across all barriers of human frailty; that we may learn compelling devotion and generous dedication of ourselves to the common good.

Our wheel of deepest blue has turned to purest gold,
The distaff missing — for the hands are cold.
Life's battles o'er, the threads no longer run,
The fabric finished — the prize for duty won.
      Author Unknown

Our Chaplain General

Ann Salley Crider
2013-2016

(from the DAR website)

The Chaplain General encourages us to … "keep in our hearts the two scriptures the President General has selected as we, the Daughters of the American Revolution, continue our work *Honoring our Heritage ~ Focusing on the Future ~ Celebrating America!*

The NSDAR Rituals and Missals which have been compiled by Past Chaplains General from contributions of many who have served as chaplains at national, state and chapter levels, are offered to the members of the National Society as a resource when needed. These rituals and prayers may be adapted as appropriate to reflect the thoughts and beliefs of the intended audience or you may write your own prayers to fit the occasion.

NSDAR respects the freedom to worship as one chooses as was established by the Founding Fathers. Chapters are always encouraged to be considerate of those who may have varying faiths."

Acknowledgments

For all of the assistance provided in the creation of this booklet I am eternally grateful. Without diligent digging and researching by Florida Honorary State Regents, Jeannette Frey and Jean Mann, Florida State Chaplain, Victoria Barnett, and archivist Rebecca Baird from the Office of Historian General, much of the information would be incomplete.

Kathleen J. Callanan, past State Librarian, FSSDAR, author and emerging genealogy expert, offered friendly suggestions and editing.

I encourage you to visit the website of the National Society. And remember to guard that which is committee to your trust.

Many of you have asked me what my favorite scripture is. I offer it as a closing benediction.

"Nothing can separate us from the love of God."
Romans 8: 39

May God bless you and God bless America

About the Author

Born in Cincinnati, Ohio, B.B. grew up in Miami, Florida. After graduating from the University of South Florida, she taught biology in the Miami Public School System. Five years later she earned her graduate degree from Emory University to become a school library media specialist. During her thirtieth year with the school system, another path opened up for her: she pursued a lifelong interest in massage therapy. Retiring from education in 2001 she achieved her goal to become a licensed massage therapist. In addition to her practice B.B. has returned to her first love of teaching and offers classes for massage students.

Her first book, *GG's Principle: Three Steps to Empower You in Any Situation*, was published in 2011. It was inspired by her late husband Gerry Gould and the ninety eight words he lived by. As a healer, author and educator, B.B. is available for motivational speaking.

B.B. is a member of the Daughters of the American Revolution, Biscayne Chapter, formerly of the Golden Anchor Chapter, where she joined from the Children of the American Revolution. She serves on the State Speakers Staff and is the VAVS representative to the Miami VA Healthcare System. Other memberships include the Florida State Massage Therapy Association, South Florida Palm Society and Fulford United Methodist Church. Known as the "punster" her hobbies include singing, gardening and swimming. B.B. shares a tropical home with her two Boston terriers, Grace and Joy.

Also by B.B. Gould

GG's Principle: Three Steps to Empower You in Any Situation

And Forgive Us Our Debts

Available on Amazon.com

www.ingramcontent.com/pod-product-compliance
Lightning Source LLC
Chambersburg PA
CBHW070749050426
42449CB00010B/2393